Bipolar Disorder, Depression, and Other Mood Disorders

Other titles in Diseases and People

—Diseases and People—

Bipolar Disorder, Depression, and Other Mood Disorders

Helen A. Demetriades

Enslow Publishers, Inc.

40 Industrial Road   PO Box 38
Box 398   Aldershot
Berkeley Heights, NJ 07922   Hants GU12 6BP
USA   UK

http://www.enslow.com

Library of Congress Cataloging-in-Publication Data

Demetriades, Helen A.
    Bipolar disorder, depression, and other mood disorders / Helen A. Demetriades.
        p. cm. -- (Diseases and people)
        Summary: Identifies the causes, symptoms, and treatment of mood disorders such as
bipolar disorder and depression, which can have environmental, genetic, or physiological
aspects.
        Includes bibliographical references and index.
        ISBN 0-7660-1898-9 (alk. paper)
        1. Affective disorders—Juvenile literature. [1. Depression, Mental.
    2. Manic-depressive illness. 3. Affective disorders.] I. Title. II. Series.
    RC537 .D412 2002
    616.85'27—dc21

                                                    2002006826

Printed in the United States of America

10 9 8 7 6 5 4 3

To Our Readers:
We have done our best to make sure all Internet Addresses in this book were active and
appropriate when we went to press. However, the author and the publisher have no control
over and assume no liability for the material available on those Internet sites or on other
Web sites they may link to. Any comments or suggestions can be sent by e-mail to
comments@enslow.com or to the address on the back cover.

Illustration Credits: Associated Press/Kevork Djansezian, p. 73; Chris Priest and
Mark Clarke/Science Photo Library, p. 33; © Corel Corporation, pp. 18, 45;
Cordelia Molloy/Science Photo Library, p. 23; Courtesy of the National Library of
Medicine, pp. 51, 63, 65, 67, 69; Díamar Interactive Corporation, pp. 13, 85;
Enslow Publishers, Inc., pp. 26 (both), 28; Gary Parker/Science Photo Library,
p. 82; John Bavosi/Science Photo Library, p. 21; Josh Sher/Science Photo Library,
p. 56; Mark Clarke/Science Photo Library, p. 14; Mauro Fermariello/Science
Photo Library, p. 77; Oscar Burriel/Science Photo Library, pp. 37, 41; Sheila
Terry/Science Photo Library, pp. 10, 46.

Cover Illustration: Oscar Burriel/Science Photo Library

Contents

MOOD DISORDERS

What are mood disorders? Mood disorders mainly involve disturbances in the person's emotional state. The two main mood disorders are major depression (extreme sadness) and mania (extreme happiness and overactivity). Mood disorders are usually episodic, which means that the sufferer experiences mood disturbances at relatively brief, distinct periods during the course of the illness.

Who gets them? People from infancy to older adulthood can develop mood disorders.

What are the causes? Studies have shown that people who have a genetic predisposition (that is, someone whose family members suffer from mood disorders) are more likely to develop mood disorders themselves. Personal and situational factors are also influential.

What occurs when mood disorders develop? In depressive episodes, feelings of extreme sadness, hopelessness, and helplessness may be expressed. In manic episodes, feelings of extreme elation or joy may be expressed. People with bipolar disorder, also called manic-depressive illness, suffer from alternating periods of depression and mania.

What are some early symptoms? Early symptoms of mood disorders can include lack of energy or enthusiasm to do the things the person once enjoyed; extreme sadness or irritability; withdrawal or isolation from friends and family members; and a drop in grades or productivity at work. Early symptoms can also include periods of extreme happiness or overactivity, which then give way to periods of extreme sadness.

How can they be prevented? Mood disorders can be prevented by identifying the triggers of a depressive or manic episode, and then restructuring the thinking that surrounds them. This is usually done with a combination of therapy and mood-stabilizing medications.

How are they treated? Mood disorders can be treated most effectively by a combination of medications and therapy. People with mood disorders typically return to normal levels of functioning after treatment.

1
The Story of Heather

Heather's alarm clock rings. It is time for her to get up and prepare for school. Heather is in the sixth grade, and today there is going to be a pep rally. Once Heather remembers the rally at school, she rolls over and thinks of how she is going to get out of another day of school. Unlike her classmates, she is not excited about the pep rally. She has not been looking forward to it, or to any day at school. Nothing seems to excite her much anymore. She would rather just be at home, alone. Heather decides that she will be "sick" again today.

For weeks now, Heather has felt as though a black cloud has been hanging over her. She just cannot seem to shake the feeling. It is as if nothing makes her happy anymore. She does not have the energy or the desire to do the things she once enjoyed. She does not know what is making her feel so blue— she just knows that this is how she feels on a regular basis.

Most people experience the symptoms of mild depression, such as sadness or despair, at some point in life. The condition is not classified as a serious illness, however, unless the person's behavior or physical state is affected, causing loss of sleep or appetite, for example.

Heather's teachers have been wondering what is happening with her. They wonder what is making her so irritable and why such a popular girl has become so isolated. They contemplate why she no longer participates in her classes the way she used to, and why her grades have been slipping. Some of Heather's teachers think that she has become lazy. Others are beginning to wonder if something else is going on.

Everyone feels sad or irritable once in a while. For Heather, it is what keeps her in bed on school days and at home alone on weekends. Heather hardly even talks to her friends on the phone now. They have stopped calling her because she was always so cranky and never wanted to be with them. She cannot understand why she has no motivation to do the things she once used to do.

Depression and related mood disorders are among the most common disorders in America today. Mood disorders are listed as one of the top ten causes of worldwide disability, with major depression ranking first.[1] Major depression affects approximately 35–45 million Americans during their lifetime.[2] More than 17 million Americans suffer from depression each year.[3]

In adulthood, nearly twice as many females are diagnosed with depression as males.[4] However, before the onset of puberty, depressive disorders appear to be equally as common in males and females.[5] Researchers estimate that the lifetime risk of major depression is approximately 10–25 percent for females, and 5–12 percent for males living in the United States.[6] About one in four females will experience depression

11

at some point in their lives. These numbers greatly increase when other mood disorders are considered.

There are a great variety of causes of mood disorders. The *etiology*, or developmental history of the illness, can be related to environmental, genetic, or physiologic influences. More commonly, mood disorders are the result of both genetic and environmental forces working together.[7]

Most cases of children and adolescents with mood disturbances go unrecognized until there is significant social or academic disruption. For instance, the depressed person may become so irritable and cranky that he or she may have frequent fights with others or have a tendency to "fly off the handle" easily. The person may become socially withdrawn, isolating him- or herself from others. Or there may be a combination of these behaviors, as in Heather's case.

The depressed student can feel so helpless that it may seem as though it is not even worth trying at school. He may lose interest in all subjects, even those that he once enjoyed. He may stop doing homework assignments and studying, and his grades may drop considerably. The student may be heard to say that he just does not care anymore.

Either one or a combination of these behaviors may indicate to the student's teachers or other school officials that something is wrong. They may decide to send a note home to the student's parents, or request a meeting with them. This sort of parent-school communication is often what marks the beginning of a process of discovery regarding what has been going on emotionally for the student. Sometimes, the family

Marked changes in school performance may indicate a mood disorder.

recognizes that the student is suffering emotionally, and they help him find professional help. But the possibility also exists for the student to get help on his own. This is a difficult step to take, but one that is well worth the effort. In any case, if the situation is handled well, the student and those who are helping him will begin to understand why he has been feeling and behaving differently.

Unfortunately, people who are suffering from some form of mood disorder are not always recognized. The person may not know that she is in need of help because she may not understand what she is experiencing. Other times, people with mood disorders may not say anything to anyone out of a fear that they are "going crazy." This attitude could not be further

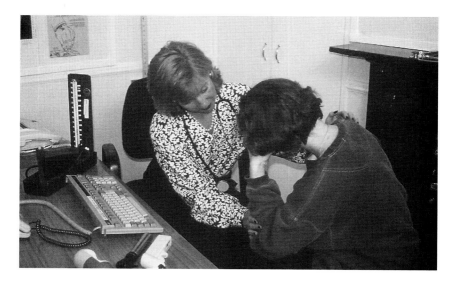

Talking with a psychologist is a good way to get help with a mood disorder.

from the truth, and such a secretive stance can have harmful consequences.

Left untreated, mood disorders can become a devastating and emotionally crippling condition. The condition can worsen until the sufferer is in need of emergency care or even hospitalization. In a worst-case scenario, the person may attempt to take his own life, potentially with tragic results.

Fortunately for Heather, there is hope. Her parents noticed the changes in her behavior and mood. They talked to her teachers, who had also become concerned. Heather's parents made an appointment for her to see a psychologist. Although Heather is a little apprehensive, she is comforted to know that help is on the way.

2

What Is a Mood Disorder?

Mood disorders are a class of disorders that are characterized by disturbances of mood or emotion. Therefore, mood disorders have at their core emotions, or feelings. *Emotion* is a word that describes a complex state of feeling.[1] What makes the state of feeling complex is that is has three main parts:

- psychological (the mental aspects of the individual);

- somatic (what is experienced physically); and

- behavioral (how the individual acts).

Mood refers to a prolonged, sustained emotion. Generally, mood is not only experienced by the individual, but can also be observed by others. Therefore, mood disturbances can affect all aspects of a person's life: work, school, thought, perception, and even health.

Mood disorders are normally episodic,[2] which means that the disturbances can increase and decrease in duration (the length of time the mood is experienced) and intensity (how strongly the emotion is felt). A person with a mood disorder may have periods of high or low intensity, followed by periods of feeling "back to normal." For example, he may feel extreme sadness for a prolonged period of time, and then feel fine. The opposite can also be true—he could feel extraordinarily happy for a time. It is also possible for a person to experience a combination of the two emotions in what is known as a *mixed state.* This is when someone has extreme highs (happiness) and extreme lows (sadness) within a relatively short period of time. When this occurs, the person may feel an inner state of tension, as if he is in a tug-of-war against himself.

Everyone experiences fluctuations, or changes, in his or her mood. This is normal. What is not normal is when the mood swings are severe, going from one extreme to another, or when a person's mood gets "stuck" in one extreme. If someone is always sad and seldom experiences joy (as in the case of Heather), this may be an indication of a mood disorder.

Causes of Mood Disorders

Mood disorders can be caused by several different factors. The most common of these include:

- stress or going through a period of change (either internal or external);
- learned helplessness;
- cognitions (thinking patterns);

- medical conditions; and
- genetics (heredity).[3]

In many cases, the cause or causes may be obvious. In others, the cause is not always clear. To further complicate matters, a person may experience any one of these possible factors individually, or in a combination of several factors together.

Stress

Stress refers to the many things in a person's life that cause mental strain or pressure. When stress becomes overwhelming, a person may begin to feel hopeless, as if there is no way out from under the burden of the stressful events. The person may also suddenly swing into action in an attempt to meet all the challenges before him, resulting in a hypomanic state, or a state of extreme excitement or action.[4]

There are four main types of stress.[5] They are:

- pressure to perform (such as having too much homework or wanting to do well during a sports event);

- frustration due to failure (not getting an important role in a play);

- conflict (two competing desires, such as wanting to excel in school and get good grades, and at the same time be popular and spend more time with friends than studying); and

- change (such as going through puberty, moving to a new town, or the loss of a loved one).

Steps to Reduce Stress

1. Take a deep breath. Hold for five or ten seconds, and then release slowly. Repeat ten times.

2. Get some exercise. Go for a walk or jog; engage in sports; go for a swim; lift weights; or participate in yoga or exercise classes.

3. Get enough sleep, but not too much. The average is about eight hours per night.

4. Eat well. Good nutrition supplies the body with the fuel it needs to perform.

5. Balance work and recreation. Too much of either will eventually stress your body and mind.

6. Reward yourself. Take time to recognize your accomplishments and treat yourself to something rewarding. Examples: Go to a movie; take a long, hot bath; take a night out with your friends; or buy a new outfit.

7. Cut large tasks into manageable pieces. Big jobs can easily become overwhelming, especially if you have several tasks to do at once. Break each task into parts that seem manageable, and then reward yourself for completing each part.

8. Set realistic goals for yourself, and come up with a plan for how to accomplish them. Recruit help when needed.

9. Make a list of the things you need to accomplish, and cross off each task when you have accomplished it.

10. Avoid alcohol and drugs.

11. Make time for friends and social activities. Talk to your friends for encouragement and support.

12. Find a quiet environment, free of distractions, where you can relax.

13. Meditate. Sit in a peaceful atmosphere and say a chosen word (such as "peace") repeatedly to yourself.

14. Find your own relaxation zone. One example may be your bedroom, where you can dim the lights and play some soft music.

15. Learn how to say "no." Taking on more responsibility or giving in to requests when you are already feeling stressed is a sure way to become overwhelmed.

Learned Helplessness

Another factor that can cause a mood disorder is the way events are learned, interpreted, and acted on.[6] Learning that inactivity, vulnerability, or dependence on others is rewarded can contribute to mood disorder. For instance, a highly controlling parent may unintentionally encourage helplessness or a lack of responsibility in his or her child. The child may then experience depression or another mood disorder.

Learned helplessness is a term that describes what happens to people who, after countless attempts, believe that their efforts do not get them anywhere.[7] In other words, a person may become hopeless in a situation that he or she sees as being uncontrollable. A person may stop studying or trying to get good grades because she may believe that her reputation for failure precedes her, and makes success impossible. This state of learned helplessness is often associated with depression.[8]

On the other hand, learning to take too much responsibility in order to be recognized, acknowledged, or attended to can also cause a mood disorder. For example, a person may feel useless unless he takes on all the tasks others cannot or will not. He may feel as though he will be rejected or unloved if he does not accept all the responsibilities he sees before him.

Cognitions

Patterns of thinking are known as *cognitions*. A person who has predominantly negative, or predominantly positive, cognitions is prone to developing an emotional disturbance. This type of thinking is common in individuals who generally view the world in "black-or-white" terms. Irrational beliefs are one type of cognition that can contribute to a mood disturbance. For example, a person may believe that he is to blame for things that are beyond his control. This is known as *catastrophizing*, or exaggerating the importance of a situation.

Medical Conditions

Medical conditions can also explain some mood disorders. Illnesses such as diabetes, acquired immunodeficiency syndrome (AIDS), and hormonal imbalances are examples of medical causes of mood disorders. Emotions are regulated by the limbic system, which is a part of the brain. Any damage to this area of the brain, such as head injury, stroke, or dementia,

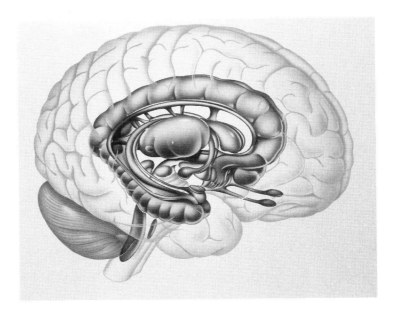

Shown here is an illustration of the limbic system of the brain. The limbic system regulates emotions in human beings.

can cause emotional disturbances. Damage to the left hemisphere, or half, of the brain is associated with depression, whereas damage to the right hemisphere can cause mania.[9]

Poor nutrition can also cause medical disorders that affect mood. For instance, a person who goes on a "crash diet" to lose weight can experience a disturbance in mood. In addition, poor sleep (either too much or too little), lack of exercise, and poor health routines can also contribute to a mood disorder.

Childbirth can trigger both biological factors (changes in the mother's body) and environmental factors (lifestyle changes) that can contribute to a mood disorder. A mood disturbance due to childbirth is known as *postpartum depression.* Normally, this type of depression lasts only a few days after giving birth. However, approximately one woman out of every 1,000 who experiences postpartum depression will develop a more serious, long-lasting depression.[10]

Biochemistry is another medical consideration that can trigger a mood disorder. There are three main biological chemicals, called *neurochemicals,* that can cause a mood disorder when they are affected.[11] These three chemicals are serotonin, norepineprine, and dopamine. When either too much or too little serotonin, norepinephrine, or dopamine are released, a disturbance of mood can occur.

Genetics

Genetics, or heredity, can predispose an individual to a mood disorder.[12] If someone in a person's family, such as a parent or grandparent, suffers from a mood disorder, then it is possible that that person may also develop a mood disorder. Often in

Some women experience postpartum depression after childbirth.

the case of an individual with a mood disorder, a *genogram*, or family tree, will help to show a family history of relatives with mood disorders. Studies have been done on identical and fraternal twins who were raised together or apart (after being separated at birth). These studies have revealed strong evidence to support the theory that heredity plays an important role in susceptibility to mood disorders.[13] Family and twin studies will be discussed in more detail in Chapter 8.

The list of causes above is by no means complete. There are times when an individual may experience a mood disorder for no apparent reason. However, it is important to make an attempt to understand the causes and history of a disorder.

By understanding the etiology, a trained medical practitioner can be better prepared to give the estimated length and amount of recovery, or *prognosis,* for the patient. Treatment options can also be enhanced by studying the etiology of the disorder.

Now that we have reviewed in general terms what mood disorders are and what their possible causes may be, we can look at the more common types of mood disorders. In addition, we can also begin to develop our understanding of the differing symptoms and severity of these mood disorders.

3

Types of Mood Disorders

I n the previous chapter, we reviewed the extreme highs (elation) and extreme lows (sadness) of mood disorders. This chapter will focus more specifically on these highs and lows, known more distinctively as depression and mania. We will also look at some of the more common types of mood disorders.

Unipolar Versus Bipolar

There are two main types of mood disorders:

- unipolar, or one end of the spectrum of mood disorders; and
- bipolar, or both ends of the spectrum.

In the spectrum on which all types of mood disorders exist, one extreme would represent disorders that include persistent sadness, very low energy, and a sense of doom. This is what is referred to as *unipolar depression*. The other extreme would

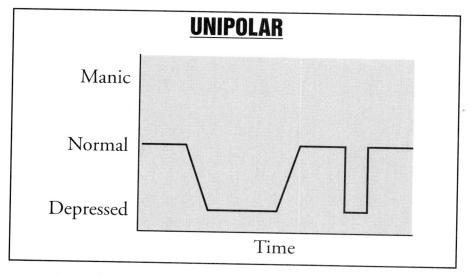

People who suffer from unipolar disorders experience depression only.

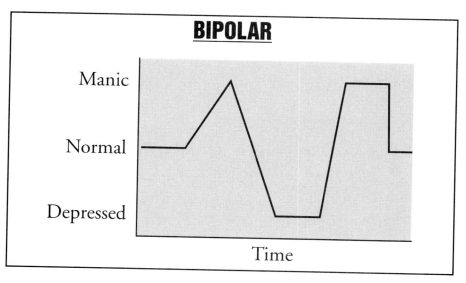

People who suffer from bipolar disorders experience both mania and depression.

represent disorders that include elation (a happy, blissful state), very high energy, and a sense that the person could take on the world. This elated state is known as *mania*. A combination of the two poles on this imaginary spectrum would cause varying degrees of both extremes. This is what is known as *bipolar disorder*.

Until now, we have mainly discussed depression, or the unipolar dimension of mood disorders. We have learned that unipolar depression can cause an individual to experience depressive episodes for shorter or longer periods of time. When a person with unipolar depression is not feeling the symptoms of depression, she generally feels "normal" again. If she is not experiencing a depressive episode, she is not likely to feel down—at least, not for a prolonged period of time. Remember, everyone has some degree of ups and downs.

Bipolar disorders are also episodic. The symptoms increase and decrease between periods of feeling emotionally stable. The difference between a bipolar disorder and a unipolar depression is that an individual with a bipolar mood disorder can go through episodes of mania followed by, combined with, or preceded by episodes of depression before feeling "normal" again. On the other hand, a person who suffers from unipolar disorder may never go though a depressive episode. Rather, he may be prone to having only episodes of mania. The existence of mania without depression has been referred to as "pure mania."[1]

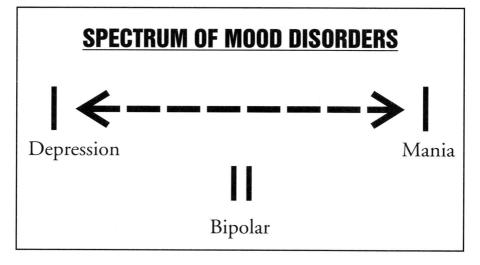

On the spectrum of mood disorders, depression lies on one end and mania lies on the other. Bipolar disorder derives symptoms from both sides.

Degrees and Types of Depression

Under the two headings of unipolar and bipolar disorders, there are several different types of disorders that range in severity.[2] On the unipolar end, the most severe type of depression is referred to as *major depressive disorder*. Symptoms must be present for at least two weeks before this diagnosis can be considered. However, the symptoms can develop in a matter of days or weeks.

A person who is experiencing a major depressive disorder may feel significant distress. She may need to put forth a greater effort than usual to do everyday things, such as making decisions, or even getting up in the morning. The person may be unable to perform her job, go to school, or even function socially when experiencing a major depressive disorder.[3]

Because of the seriousness of this disorder, the risk of suicide is high while a person is suffering from major depression. Suicide estimates are as high as 15 percent of depressed individuals.[4] Major depressive disorders explain approximately 20 to 35 percent of all suicidal deaths.[5]

Approximately 50–60 percent of people who experience one major depressive episode will have a second episode.[6] The likelihood of individuals with this disorder experiencing additional episodes increases dramatically with each episode.[7] Therefore, more frequent and longer-lasting episodes can occur—especially if the depressions are not treated.

In Chapter 1, we were introduced to the case of "Heather." If Heather were to seek professional help, she would most likely be diagnosed with major depressive disorder. Her symptoms correspond with such a diagnosis and, according to the story, she has exhibited these symptoms for several weeks—or long enough for her grades to drop significantly.

A chronic form of depression is called dysthymic disorder, or *dysthymia*. Although typically less severe, dysthymia generally lasts longer than major depression. In order to be diagnosed with dysthymia, the characteristic symptoms must be present for at least two years (one year for children and adolescents).

These two types of depression are not exclusive. An individual can experience a major depression or dysthymia separately, or they can occur together. When two disorders exist at the same time, they are called *comorbid*. The existence of major depression and dysthymia together is sometimes referred to as "double depression."[8] Estimates reveal that approximately 40 percent of people with major depressive disorder also have dysthymic disorder.[9]

Degrees and Types of Bipolar Disorders

The most severe form of bipolar disorder is called Bipolar I Disorder.[10] At its worst, bipolar disorder includes severe periods of mania alone or combined with severe depression. Suicide rates are high for those with Bipolar I Disorder. In fact, 10 percent of those with Bipolar I succeed in taking their own lives.[11]

Unlike major depression, which may only occur one time in a person's life, Bipolar I is recurrent.[12] More than 90 percent of those with Bipolar I Disorder have more than one

BIPOLAR MOOD DISORDER COMPARISON CHART			
	BIPOLAR I	BIPOLAR II	CYCLOTHYMIA
1.	Episodes of major depression	Episodes of major depression	Depressive symptoms
2.	Episodes of mania	Episodes of hypomania	Hypomanic symptoms

Symptoms must be present for at least two years (or one year for children or adolescents)

episode of mania.[13] In addition, approximately 60–70 percent of manic episodes are preceded or followed by episodes of major depression.[14]

Psychotic features may also be present in a Bipolar I Disorder. Psychotic features include having *hallucinations* (seeing things that are not there) or *delusions* (believing irrational things to be true). An example of a hallucination would be hearing voices that no one else can hear. An example of a delusion would be a person thinking that her teacher is really an alien who wants to kidnap her.

A less severe form of bipolar disorder is known as Bipolar II Disorder. This form of bipolar disorder includes many of the same symptoms as Bipolar I Disorder, but instead of experiencing full-blown manic episodes, a person with Bipolar II Disorder will undergo *hypomania*, or less severe forms of mania. A state of hypomania does not include psychotic features and does not impair a person's ability to function as drastically as a state of mania does. Others may notice and be concerned with the erratic behavior of a person experiencing hypomania, and the risk of suicide is still high (occurring in 10–15 percent of individuals with Bipolar II).[15] It is important to note that people who suffer from this form of bipolar disorder can still experience major depressive episodes, and the potential for rapid cycling (more episodes per year) is greater than in people who suffer from Bipolar I.[16]

An even less severe form of bipolar mood disorder is called *cyclothymic disorder*.[17] As in dysthymic disorder, the symptoms of cyclothymic disorder need to be present for at least two years in order to be able to diagnose someone formally with cyclothymia (one year in children and adolescents). Cyclothymia consists of hypomanic symptoms combined with, followed by, or preceded by depressive symptoms. Unlike in Bipolar II Disorder, people who experience cyclothymia generally do not have full-blown major depressive episodes.[18]

Other Types of Mood Disorders

There are two other types of mood disorders that have to do with physiology, or the biological workings of the body.[19] One is referred to as a "mood disorder due to a general medical condition." This involves a biological disorder or medical condition that may cause fluctuations in a person's mood. For example, diabetes can cause mood swings because the person may become depressive or manic, or experience hypomanic episodes or symptoms. Although this type of mood disturbance is related to physiology, the sufferer may be unable to function at his or her job, in school, or socially.

For diagnostic purposes, there must be evidence of the symptoms relating directly to the physiological condition. This could require a full medical examination, lab tests, and background history of the patient. Each of these factors must be considered and weighed before there can be an accurate diagnosis.

The other type of mood disorder that has to do with physiology is called "substance-induced mood disorder." In the case of a substance-induced mood disorder, the emotional

Before there can be an accurate diagnosis of a mood disorder, a medical examination and lab tests should be performed.

disturbance is directly related to a substance, such as street drugs or alcohol. Some medications can also cause emotional disturbances. In this case, the medications need to be altered, changed, or monitored by the prescribing doctor.

A substance-induced mood disorder can produce symptoms of depression, mania, hypomania, or a combination of the three. Like other mood disorders, a substance-induced mood disorder can cause significant impairment in social, occupational, and overall functioning. This type of mood disorder also requires supporting evidence that the disturbance is a direct result of the substance use. This evidence can be gathered from medical examinations, lab results, and historical information.

A case illustration of a substance-induced mood disorder is that of an alcoholic (someone who abuses alcohol regularly). Many people drink to "feel happy," or to lose their inhibitions. As with all drugs, alcohol alters the body's chemistry, which is what is first experienced as a "buzz," or a feeling of being drunk. However, with continued drinking over time, the alterations in the body's chemistry begin to work against the individual, resulting in a mood disorder. For this reason, alcoholics who are not in recovery are typically irritable and moody, and can exhibit symptoms either on the depressive side, the manic side, or both. Along with this emotional instability, they can also display impaired functioning in most—if not all—areas of life.

The preceding was an overview of several different mood disorders. Up until now, the symptoms of these disorders have been presented in general terms. In the next chapter, we will examine these symptoms more closely and develop a more in-depth understanding of them.

Symptoms and Diagnosis

In 1952, the first *Diagnostic and Statistical Manual of Mental Disorders* (DSM) was published by the American Psychiatric Association. The DSM was one of the first books of its kind that classified symptoms and disorders— before it was published, diagnoses (the method health care professionals use for distinguishing one illness from another) had been vague and informal. The DSM provided not only clear diagnoses for many mental illnesses, but also provided differential diagnoses, which highlighted the differences between disorders in an effort to draw a definite distinction between two similar disorders.

Today, the *Diagnostic and Statistical Manual of Mental Disorders, Fourth Edition, Text Revision* (DSM-IV-TR) is in use. This manual was revised in the year 2000. With each new revision, the information in it has become more precise.

In the DSM-IV-TR, the symptoms for each mood disorder are clearly defined. By using the symptom lists for each individual diagnosis, a trained professional is able to make differential diagnoses based on what the individual presents as his or her complaints, or by what *symptoms* (signs that something is wrong) are present.

There are many symptoms associated with mood disorders. Unipolar and bipolar mood disturbances have several symptoms in common because bipolar disorders involve depression. However, bipolar disorders also have additional symptoms that are not seen in unipolar depressions. More specifically, bipolar disorders have unique symptoms that are associated with manic episodes.

Symptoms Associated With Depressive Episodes

Hopelessness and Helplessness

Two of the main symptoms of depression are a feeling of hopelessness and a feeling of helplessness. *Hopelessness* refers to a feeling of despair, or a sense that things will never get better or seem brighter again. This sense of hopelessness can also be experienced as a sadness that cannot be shaken. *Helplessness* refers to a state of feeling unable to do anything about what is happening. This feeling of helplessness can be directed internally (unable to control emotions) or externally (unable to control outside situations and circumstances).

The main symptoms of depression are feelings of hopelessness and helplessness.

Pessimism

Often, a pessimistic attitude is associated with the feelings of hopelessness and helplessness.[1] *Pessimism* is a negative outlook on past, present, or future events. Excessive or inappropriate guilt may also accompany these feelings—a sufferer may feel that he or she is to blame for "everything." This type of thinking can reach delusional proportions; for example, an individual may believe that she is personally responsible for homelessness in America.

Worthlessness

A sense of worthlessness is another symptom that can be exhibited in a depressed state. The term *worthless* refers to the idea that an individual is useless or is not deserving of attention or affection. Often, excessive and inappropriate guilt goes along with this sense of worthlessness.[2] After all, if a person thought himself to be useful and valuable, then it is unlikely that he would feel guilt to delusional proportions over events that he views as his responsibility.

All these states—hopelessness, helplessness, pessimism, worthlessness, and guilt—correspond with an overall sense of doom. Often, this sense of doom is reflected in a person's tendency to *catastrophize*, which means to exaggerate the negative aspects of a situation without acknowledging the positive aspects.[3] For example, a person might fail an exam during a semester and then believe that she will never graduate, get a job, or be able to afford to live on her own. It would be more realistic, and healthy, to be able to acknowledge the test as only one failed test that can be made up for with future accomplishments. That single event does not need to negatively affect all aspects of life.

Anhedonia

Anhedonia, or a loss of interest or pleasure in almost everything, is another common feature of depression. Anhedonia applies to things that were once found interesting or pleasurable, such as playing a particular sport or hanging out with friends. Anhedonia, especially in combination with other symptoms, can frequently lead to social withdrawal or isolation.

Social Withdrawal

Social withdrawal occurs when the desire to be with or around others is no longer experienced.[4] An individual who is becoming withdrawn may find himself coming up with one excuse after another to avoid being in social situations. Family outings or parties with friends may become a source of dread. Eventually, the socially withdrawn person may become isolated, and find himself with no one he considers to be a friend. He may feel that he cannot count on anyone, and may experience a deep sense of being alone and misunderstood.

Another symptom that can contribute to social isolation is increased *irritability*, or a continuous cranky mood. One way that irritability can be expressed is by frequent outbursts of anger. Another display of irritability is a low frustration tolerance, which commonly leads to more angry outbursts, social withdrawal, helplessness, and so on. Depression can quickly become a downward spiral, or a vicious cycle that repeats itself.

Once a person becomes depressed, each of these symptoms can build on the other, bringing the person deeper and deeper into a sense of despair.

Anxiety

Symptoms of *anxiety*, such as fear, worry, apprehension, and general nervousness, may also be present. This is especially true for children and adolescents, who may exhibit depressive symptoms differently.[5] For example, social anxieties may be observed, and can eventually lead to social withdrawal and/or isolation. Anxiety may also be expressed by frequent stomach aches, headaches, and general aches and pains.

Sleep and Appetite Disturbances

Sleep and appetite disturbances are other common features of mood disorders. Alterations in sleep patterns can indicate a problem—too much or too little sleep can be symptoms of a mood disturbance.[6] Too much sleep is known as *hypersomnia*, and too little sleep is called *insomnia*. In addition, changes to sleep patterns can occur. For instance, a person may sleep during the day but not at all at night. Trouble falling asleep, restless sleep, and waking early are other types of sleep disturbances.

Appetite changes can also involve patterns of too much or too little. Overeating can occur, adding up to several meals and snacks daily. Overeating can also involve eating the same number of meals as always, but consuming larger portions at each meal. Undereating can occur in a similar fashion. A decrease in the number of meals or a decrease in the portions

Frequent headaches may be a sign of anxiety.

of each meal can be problematic. This is especially true if the appetite changes are not planned, as in deciding to go on a diet to lose weight, but occur unintentionally. These appetite changes are often accompanied by significant weight loss or gain in a short period of time. In general, a rise or drop in weight by more than ten pounds in approximately three to six months can be a symptom of an appetite disturbance.

Decreased Energy

Decreased energy is another feature of depression. Often, people who suffer from depression feel as though they are always tired. Likewise, they feel that they have trouble mustering the energy to complete tasks, making even simple things like doing homework or paying bills seem daunting and overwhelming. *Psychomotor retardation* (looking and feeling slow and sluggish) or *psychomotor agitation* (feeling physically agitated or restless) may also be experienced.

Depression can interfere with a person's ability to concentrate, make decisions, remember, and think. A person suffering from depression may suddenly find it difficult to understand material presented in class, even though it may be a subject she excelled in previously. Or she may have trouble making everyday decisions, such as what to wear in the morning. People with depression may feel as though their heads are in a fog and that they simply cannot think clearly. They may have trouble remembering something that just happened. It is easy to imagine how frustrating this can be for someone who never experienced any of these problems before.

In addition, recurring thoughts of death are often present in depression. The frequency and intensity of these thoughts can vary greatly. For instance, a person who suffers from depression may think that others would be better off without him. Or he may believe that he would not be missed, and question the point of living. He may view death as the only option to stop the pain he is feeling. Suicidal thoughts, plans, or actions are consistent with the tendency to catastrophize in that the person's ability to view the greater picture is severely impaired.

Symptoms Associated With Manic Episodes

Euphoria and Mood Lability

Manic episodes generally look like the opposite of depressive episodes. Rather than persistent sadness, manic episodes are marked by a state of expansive, elevated mood.[7] The elevated mood may reach a state of *euphoria,* or extreme elation. A person in a manic state may seem "too happy" or cheerful. A manic episode can be experienced as an extended high. At first, the sufferer may enjoy the feeling of a manic episode. However, those who know the person will recognize that something is not right. Mood *lability,* or instability, is also common. Frequently, lability will involve rapid shifts in mood from euphoric to irritable, especially when the person's goals are thwarted.[8]

Grandiosity

Along with these alterations in mood, an inflated sense of self-worth, or *grandiosity*, may be present. Grandiosity can reach delusional proportions. An example of a grandiose sense of self is the belief that any feat can be accomplished, no matter how impossible it may seem. For instance, a person suffering from grandiosity may believe that she can build an amusement park, despite having no education, knowledge, or experience in building one. Grandiosity can also entail someone who credits him- or herself with more than is deserved. For example, a person might believe that he has a special relationship with God or a supreme being who speaks or otherwise deals directly with him, and has selected him for a special purpose.

Optimism

Along with a grandiose sense of self and an elevated mood, an optimistic outlook is characteristically present. This is reflected in a person's belief that this is the best world possible, or that there can only be favorable outcomes in whatever he or she does. This is unlike a depressive state, in which a pessimistic outlook is most common; however, a negative outlook may be present in a manic state—a person may believe that the world is doomed unless they are saved by the manic individual's "special powers."

Sleep and Appetite Disturbances

As in depressive episodes, manic episodes also involve sleep disturbances. However, in a manic state, the sleep disturbance

A person suffering from grandiosity may believe that he has a special relationship with God or a supreme being. (Shown here is a detail of "Il Creatore," from the ceiling of the Sistine Chapel.)

is typically in one direction. Generally, sleeplessness or a decreased need for sleep is experienced. Individuals suffering from a manic episode may feel that sleep is a waste of time. They may get as little as two hours of sleep nightly, and still feel rested (in truth, even though the individual may feel rested, this is not a sufficient amount of sleep—the body requires approximately eight hours of sleep per night). Appetite disturbances can also be present, because the person may feel as though eating will only slow him or her down.

Sleep disturbances can be present in someone who is suffering from a manic episode.

Hyperactivity

A heightened level of energy, known as hyperactivity, is typically present in manic episodes.[9] As in depressive episodes, this can involve psychomotor agitation or restlessness. The person experiencing a manic episode may become involved in several projects at once. He may become hyper-social, calling friends at all hours of the night without regard for the time. He may engage in countless social activities. In addition, he may dominate social activities, such as conversations, and not give others a chance to participate. This type of behavior can

46

place a strain on friendships, especially because the manic individual is unaware of how inappropriate he is being.

The manic individual's speech may also be affected. She may talk rapidly, or with pressured speech. She may be more talkative than usual, and her volume may be loud, making it difficult for anyone to interrupt. She may tend to make more jokes or puns than normal, even when it is inappropriate to do so.[10] If the individual is experiencing an irritable mood, her speech may be dominated by aggressive, hostile, or complaining outbursts.

Dramatic or theatrical behavior may be present in both speech and mannerisms. For example, a person experiencing a manic episode may sing his thoughts instead of merely saying them. Grand hand movements and facial expressions are also typically present.

Racing Thoughts

Racing thoughts are frequently experienced in a manic episode.[11] This can involve a *flight of ideas*, which means that the person's thoughts are hard to follow due to frequent topic changes in conversation. What makes this flight of ideas worse is that only the manic individual is aware that she is changing the topic, and listeners are left to guess what the relevance is to the previous topic. This can lead to aggravation and frustration on both parts. Racing thoughts and flight of ideas contribute to rapid speech because the ideas are hitting faster than the individual can say them aloud. In its most extreme form, the individual may become *incoherent*, or not understandable to those around her.

Disorganization and Distractibility

Disorganization and distractibility can also be present in a manic episode. Frequent shifts in thought content (what the individual is thinking) along with an inability to screen incoming information can be quite difficult to deal with. Frequent shifts in thinking and attention can lead a manic individual to become highly disorganized and distracted.

Impulsivity

The final symptom of manic episodes is *impulsivity*, or the inability to think things through and consider the consequences before acting. When things are not thought through, judgment can become impaired. Examples of impulsive behaviors are:

- buying/spending sprees;
- recklessness; and
- sexual indiscretion.

Impulsivity holds the potential for self-damaging behaviors and severe consequences.

This chapter focused on the diagnosis and symptoms of mood disorders. The classic symptoms of both depressive and manic episodes have been reviewed. We have learned how unsettling each of the symptoms can be, not only for the individuals experiencing them, but also for others around the sufferer. However, like our case example of Heather, who was presented in the first chapter, there is hope for recovery. In the next chapter, we will look at treatments for mood disorders.

Treatment of Mood Disorders

5

When an individual is suffering from a mood disorder, things can look pretty ominous. It may seem as though the person may never return to his former self again. Fortunately, with the help of professionals who are familiar with mood disorders, there is hope. Treatment options are many and varied.[1] Together with their health care providers, people who suffer from mood disorders can choose the treatment best suited for their particular needs.

Treatment of a psychological disorder depends on the etiology of the mood disorder. As mentioned in Chapter 3, a thorough history and assessment are necessary to understand the etiology. A physical examination and lab work may also be required.

There are hundreds of different therapy and treatment options today. Most of these treatments for mood disorders can fit into one of three generic categories:

- insight therapies;
- behavior therapies; or
- biomedical techniques.

Each of these methods can be used alone or in a combination of two or three. Often, a combination of these approaches is used to gain the best results in the shortest amount of time. However, this is not always the best solution.

Insight Therapies

Insight therapy involves talking to a trained professional in an effort to gain understanding and *insight*, or self-knowledge, into the sufferer's feelings and experiences. This type of treatment is often referred to as *psychodynamic*, or exploratory, therapy.[2]

Although there are modern approaches to this type of therapy, the classic version involves delving into childhood or past issues in an effort to uncover unconscious conflicts (conflicts that the sufferer may not even realize he or she has). Dr. Sigmund Freud, a physician who lived from 1856–1939, is credited as being the first to develop a comprehensive model of psychoanalysis.[3] In his model, Freud focused on conflict and the unconscious.

According to Freud, *conflict* is the term that is used to describe two competing forces. Conflicts occur between the *id* (the primitive part of the mind that wants instant gratification for desires and needs) and the *superego* (the guilt-producing part of the mind, or the conscience).[4] The *ego* is what

Dr. Sigmund Freud is credited as being the first to develop a comprehensive model of psychoanalysis.

mediates, or tries to form a compromise, between the id and the superego. An example of this type of conflict is wanting a triple scoop of ice cream (the id's desire) while trying to watch your diet (the superego's restraint). In the end, you might decide to have a single scoop or a frozen yogurt (the ego's compromise). When either the id or the superego becomes too powerful, the individual may begin to show symptoms of a manic state (the id becoming too powerful) or a depressive state (the superego becoming too powerful).

The unconscious describes all the information that is stored in our minds but that we are not always aware of. This information can be difficult to access. The information stored in the unconscious includes all our memories, thoughts, and desires from the past and present that we are not currently aware of. The unconscious begins to develop at birth (some might argue that development begins even earlier). It has been thought that the unconscious is what drives behavior.

An example of unconscious memory is that of having been a child, left alone by your parents for a long enough time to have caused fear and the worry that you were abandoned or forgotten. If this fear is not dealt with appropriately, the memory could, in time, develop into a fear of abandonment. This could result in you becoming clingy—never wanting to let people go out of fear that they will leave you forever. The opposite could also be true—you could push people away and never develop a closeness with them in an effort to ward off the possibility of being forgotten. Your behavior would be driven by this unconscious memory. In terms of a mood disorder, we could draw this example out even further by saying that any future abandonment (either real or perceived) could reawaken this childhood memory. As a result, the individual may become depressed due to feelings of loss, rejection, worthlessness, or the like. In addition, the individual may feel helpless against this perceived pattern of abandonment.

Insight-oriented treatment would therefore focus on uncovering this "original trauma," or memory of a bad event. The theory is that once the memory is uncovered, examined, and understood, the individual could then resolve the painful feelings associated with the memory and then move on. Additionally, any unresolved conflicts hidden within the unconscious would also be discovered and worked through. Insight would be achieved.

Behavior Therapies

Behavior therapy focuses on the individual's behaviors in an effort to change experiences.[5] The main premise of this therapy is that an understanding of human behavior should be based only on what can be observed. There is no need to discuss conflict or the unconscious; instead, what is focused on is learned behavior. B. F. Skinner (1904–1990), an American psychologist who was best known for his research into the learning process, is credited with being a forerunner of behaviorism as applied to human psychology.

Behaviorists' view of human behavior is simply stated: What has been learned can be unlearned. Therefore, the behaviorist view of mood disorders is that the symptoms represent *maladaptive,* or unsuitable, behaviors that were learned. In other words, it is believed that the individual can be taught new, adaptive behaviors to correct what he or she has previously learned.

Cognitive-behavioral approaches take the main theories of behaviorism one step further by acknowledging things that cannot be observed.[6] Cognitive behaviorists recognize mental events, such as faulty cognitions (the persistent thought, "I cannot do anything right"), examine them, and replace them with more accurate ones.[7] In cognitive-behavioral approaches, what an individual is thinking plays an important part in which behaviors are developed and which are not.

A behaviorist would likely look at Heather, from the case example in Chapter 1, in her home and school environment in an effort to study the maladaptive behavior in question: Heather's depressive symptoms. A general pattern of behavior would likely emerge after examining the *antecedents*, or what occurs just before the behavior that is being studied, and the *consequences*, or what occurs just after the behavior is observed.

A typical scenario might be that each time Heather is in some way rejected (the antecedent), she becomes sad and withdrawn (the maladaptive behavior). And each time she becomes sad and withdrawn, she gets lots of attention (the consequence). After a while, this pattern will cause Heather's symptoms to worsen until a full-blown depression exists. Before she knows it, Heather will prefer to remain in bed on an important school day, claiming to be sick and feeling too depressed to attend school.

A behaviorist treating Heather would probably examine the antecedents, the maladaptive behavior, and the consequences. He would then attempt to reorganize the parts of the system so that the maladaptive behavior is no longer encouraged or reinforced in any way. He would then try to encourage more positive, or adaptive, behaviors. If all this was accomplished, and school and family members were cooperative, then Heather would be feeling better in just a matter of time.

Biomedical Therapies

Biomedical approaches seek to reduce the symptoms of mood disorders at the physiological level. Unlike the two types of treatments previously mentioned, insight and behavioral therapies, biomedical approaches focus only on how the individual's body chemistry functions.

Drug therapy and electroconvulsive (shock) therapy (ECT) are the two most common biomedical approaches used today.[8] Although there are other biomedical approaches that are also used, we will focus on the two most common in this chapter.

Drug Therapy

Drug therapy is also known as *psychopharmacologic intervention*, or *psychopharmacotherapy*. Broken down, psychopharmacotherapy describes treatment (therapy) for mental disorders (psycho) with medication (pharmaco). There are many medications that are currently on the market to help treat mood disorders.[9] Some of these have been around longer than others, and new ones are introduced nearly every year. Many of the older medications have also been improved to cause fewer side effects and faster results.

As there are two main types of mood disorders—unipolar and bipolar—there are also two main types of drug treatment. One is specifically used to help relieve the symptoms of depression, and the other is specifically used to help bipolar mood disorders. They are both used to reduce the symptoms of an ongoing episode, and to prevent future episodes.

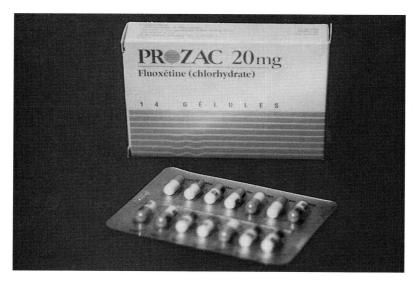

Antidepressants produce elevations in mood and fight the symptoms of depression.

Antidepressants

Antidepressant drugs are generally used for unipolar depressions. Although the various antidepressants work differently chemically speaking, they all serve the same purpose. Antidepressants produce elevations in mood and fight the symptoms of depression. In general, antidepressants work successfully in about 80 percent of depressed individuals.[10]

Mood Stabilizers

Mood stabilizers are used for bipolar mood disorders. They work by evening out mood swings and treating the symptoms of both mania and depression. Lithium was the first of these to be introduced to the market.[11] Lithium was originally a sensation to long-time sufferers, but it had its problems. Severe side effects were detected with the use of Lithium, which required the patient to be closely monitored while taking the medication. In addition, frequent blood tests had to be performed. Fortunately, Lithium has been improved since it first appeared. In addition, there are now other mood stabilizers to choose from that have fewer side effects and are less difficult to monitor.

Electroconvulsive Therapy (ECT)

Another popular biomedical approach is electroconvulsive therapy, or ECT. Although ECT was first discovered to aid in the symptoms of schizophrenia (a severe mental disorder that is characterized by unpredictable disturbances in thinking), it is most commonly used today for severe depressions. Surprisingly, ECT is not fully understood. What is known is that ECT works by producing a mild seizure in the *cortex*, or the outermost part of the brain. However, exactly how this alleviates symptoms of depression is not known. It is for this reason that the use of ECT is highly controversial. Still, it has proved to be an effective treatment.

As previously mentioned, ECT is used as a last resort option for the most severe forms of depression and mania.[12] It is a last resort for two reasons: First, it is not fully understood, and is therefore controversial. Second, ECT can cause serious side effects. Therefore, it becomes a treatment choice only after all other options have been exhausted. Nonetheless, it is estimated that over 100,000 people receive ECT every year[13] due to its high rate of effectiveness.[14]

All three of these treatments (insight, behavioral, and biomedical) can be—and often are—used simultaneously. This is referred to as a *biopsychosocial* approach, which is the consideration of all the factors involved in treating a mood disorder.[15]

Broken down, the word biopsychosocial describes investigating, understanding, and treating the biological workings of the individual (bio), the psychological makeup of the individual (psycho), and the social environment of the individual (social). Everything pertaining to the individual is taken into account, and nothing is taken for granted. Because people in general are complicated and unique, using a biopsychosocial approach appears most sensible. It is for this reason that the biopsychosocial approach is the current trend in mental health.

This chapter was dedicated to a discussion of modern treatment approaches. However, treatment was not always so available, nor were mood disorders as understood as they are today. In the next chapter, we will take a trip back in time and look at the history and development of mood disorders.

6

The History of Mood Disorders

This chapter is devoted to looking at a historical account of mood disorders. Unfortunately, because mood disorders were not understood in the past as well as they are now, it is difficult to discuss this class of disorders as a distinct entity. Therefore, we will review a historical account of mental illnesses.

Mental Illness and Its Determinants

Mental illness refers to the various disorders or afflictions of the mind that cause abnormal behavior. What is considered to be abnormal behavior depends on several different factors. These factors include:

- deviance;
- personal distress;
- maladaptive behavior; and
- current political and scientific trends.[1]

Deviance

Deviance relates to what is currently normal within society. Basically, when a person departs in some way from what is considered normal within any particular culture, it is considered to be deviant behavior. For example, having multiple body piercings and tattoos might be considered deviant in some parts of the United States. Often, deviance is associated with maladaptive behavior and is considered to be problematic.

Personal Distress

When a person is suffering from a depressive episode, a great amount of emotional pain can be experienced. *Personal distress* relates to the discomfort or pain an individual is feeling that can be communicated to others.

Maladaptive Behaviors

If an individual's adaptive functioning is impaired, it is considered to be maladaptive behavior. For example, Heather from the case example in Chapter 1 became unable to perform adaptively, socially and at school. We know this because her grades dropped, she was no longer interested in social situations, and her friendships had become strained and problematic. From these examples, it can be determined that her behavior had become maladaptive.

Current Political and Scientific Trends

Current political and scientific trends are considered to be factors of what is considered normal versus abnormal behavior.

These trends are related to what is normal within a culture or society. For example, it used to be considered politically (and legally) acceptable to own another human being as a slave. However, not only would this same behavior be seen today as unlawful, it would also be viewed as cruel and socially intolerable. Therefore, it is no longer a politically acceptable act, and someone who expresses the desire to own a slave would be considered deviant.

Likewise, recent scientific discoveries have led our nation to look down on cigarette smoking. This was not always the case, however. Not only was smoking once the norm, but it was also a sign of etiquette and status. For example, in the past, it was regular practice to be greeted by a medical practitioner in his or her private office or in the hospital with a cigarette in hand! Today, this would be considered legally irresponsible, unsanitary, and therefore abnormal behavior.

The Historical Development of Mental Illness

Mental illness has existed since the beginning of recorded history.[2] However, the phrase, "mental illness," is a modern one. Before the widespread use of this term, terms such as "lunatic," "maniac," "crazy," "mad," and "insane" were used to describe individuals with any form of mental illness. These terms are not considered proper today.[3]

The explanations of mental illness that have been offered throughout time can be placed into three main categories. They include:

- the supernatural;

- the biological; and

- the psychological.[4]

During any particular time in history, each of the following explanations weighed more or less heavily based on the factors of what was considered abnormal behavior.

The Supernatural

Supernatural explanations of mental illness have been offered since the beginning of time. Generally speaking, this view held that evil or mysterious forces entering the mind or body are what cause mental illness. Did you know that saying "bless you" after someone sneezes comes from this theory? It was once believed that a person was open to evil spirits entering the body when he or she sneezed!

During the Stone Ages (a period of time when people used stone, rather than metal, tools), there were methods of curing illnesses that developed out of ignorance. For example, evidence of trephination exists dating back to the stone ages.[5] *Trephination* is an unsophisticated technique in which a hole is made in a person's skull in an attempt to release the "evil spirits" inside. Just imagine the tools they used back then—rocks, branches, and spears!

Religious beliefs have also been used to explain illnesses.[6] Practices such as ceremonial blessings have been used for centuries. *Exorcism*, or the removal of "evil spirits" by prayer and blessing, was the preferred treatment during the Middle

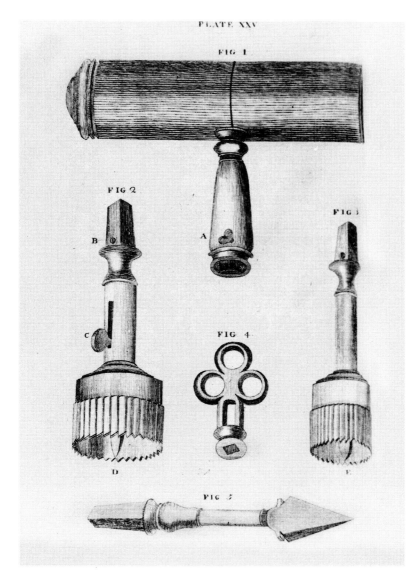

PLATE XXV

FIG 1

FIG 2

FIG 3

FIG 4

FIG 5

Primitive people viewed trephination, or the process of drilling holes in people's heads, as a valid medical procedure. The above illustration shows some equipment used in the practice of trephination.

Ages (A.D. 1000–1450).[7] Witch-hunts became popular during the Renaissance (A.D. 1450–1600).[8] During a witch-hunt, people who were accused of practicing witchcraft were tortured or put to death. This was done in an effort to ease society's suspicions that "witches" were summoning evil spirits and causing people to be ill. Witch-hunts were repeated in 1692 in Salem, Massachusetts, and again in 1782 in Glarus, Switzerland.[9]

The Biological

Generally speaking, this explanation of mental illness holds physiological malfunctioning to be of primary importance. This would include any influence that the body has over the psychic mind that would cause a manic episode, a depressive episode, or both.

The biological explanation dates back to ancient times. Methods such as herbal remedies, hot spring and mineral baths, and massage were used in an effort to "ease the mind" and cure the ailment. Unpleasant remedies, such as bleeding a patient with leeches or by other means, were also used.

Hippocrates (460?–370? B.C.), a well-known ancient physician who is known as the father of medicine, was one of the first to apply a medical model to mental illness. He is credited as being the first to assume that all illnesses, mental and physical, had a biological foundation.[10] Specifically related to mental illness, Hippocrates thought that abnormal behavior was due to irregularities in the brain or body.

Hippocrates' example became the standard in medicine. Throughout time, his theory has been applied to many

Hippocrates was one of the first physicians to believe that all illnesses had
a biological foundation.

different illnesses. Unfortunately, scientific explanations of abnormal behavior often fell short due to inadequate scientific research and understanding. For example, a type of mental illness known as hysterical neurosis was once thought to be an affliction that only occurred in women, caused by a wandering uterus within the body. Now, not only is this type of mental illness known to apply to both males and females, but science has also shown that it is impossible for a uterus to "wander" or move around within the body. Surprisingly, though, this idea only dates back to just over 100 years ago. Fortunately, the scientific community has achieved a much greater understanding of mental illness in more recent years.

The Psychological

Psychological explanations of mental illness are the most recent of the explanations to be offered. The category of psychological explanations includes all matters of the mind that pertain to a person's psychic and emotional life. Psychological explanations offer clarification of how an individual's mental status directs behavior.

In looking at these historical explanations of mental illness, it is not hard to see how misunderstood abnormal behavior has been over time. It is equally plain to see that the past understanding of what mental illness is limited treatment approaches and rendered them inadequate. In fact, treatment of the mentally ill was frequently inhumane until only recently.

The History of Treatment

Until the 1700s, the mentally ill were normally banished from society, tortured, maimed, and even killed.[11] When they were banished, they were usually either exiled to a remote area to live in seclusion, or they were placed in an insane asylum. Once in an asylum, their treatment was harsh and regularly included being chained. Eventually, a few courageous scholars began to speak up against the cruel treatment of the mentally ill.

Dr. Philippe Pinel was one of the first doctors of the late 1700s to believe that his mentally ill patients were not morally defective, but were suffering from a medical condition.

In the 1800s, a movement was made to separate those who were criminals from those who were mentally ill. This was done because abnormal behavior was beginning to be recognized as an illness, rather than as an act that should be punished. Along with this newfound acknowledgment of mental illness came better treatment for the mentally ill, but mental illness was still far from being understood.[12]

It was not until the late 1800s that a list of mental disorders was devised by Emil Kraepelin.[13] In it, this "manual" of mental disorders included a classification system that was based on what caused symptoms of mental illness, treatment, and the physiological aspects of the various disorders. This was an important advance in differentiating among the various mental illnesses. Kraepelin's classification system was not replaced until the *Diagnostic and Statistical Manual* was published in 1952.

In 1879, the first laboratory for psychology was developed.[14] Then, in 1896, the first psychology clinic was created.[15] Here, individuals with mental illness could be treated and studied. By the turn of the century, efforts were being made to recognize, differentiate, treat, and study mental illness appropriately and systematically.[16]

Today, although our understanding is not yet complete—and may never be—it has certainly come a long way. Symptoms of mental illnesses and differential diagnoses are better appreciated. People who suffer from mental illness are no longer treated inhumanely. Treatment options are many and varied. In addition, sufferers of mental illness are educated

In the late 1800s, Emil Kraepelin, one of the most influential German psychiatrists of his time, developed a classification system for mental disorders.

about their particular illness(es) and are asked to take an active role in their treatment, if possible. Although sufferers of mental illness still have an uphill battle to fight (not just individually, but in society), those with mood disorders can find hope in the progress being made in the field of mental health.

7
Mood Disorders, Society, and Culture

The *prevalence*, or percentage of a population that exhibits a disorder during a certain time period, of mood disorders has grown over the years.[1] This is partially due to the correct labeling of the disorder. It is also due to society's "acceptance" of mood disorders. What was once considered to be a sign of personal weakness or laziness is slowly being recognized as a condition that a person needs help to overcome. In addition, the prevalence has increased due to the high demands and stress that individuals in American society have adopted. Many people often feel helpless in the face of endless expectations to perform and produce.

Stereotypes and Myths

Society has not fully accepted mood disorders, or mental illness in general. There are still many stereotypes and myths that exist. As discussed in the previous chapter, although society as a whole has certainly come a long way, negative attitudes still persist.

The term *stereotype* is usually defined as "a metal printing plate case from a mold made from set type." Applied socially, stereotypes refer to the attribution of certain characteristics to individuals who share membership in a particular group. Thus, those with mood disorders would stereotypically be lumped together as one whole group, and afforded various characteristics based on their group membership. It is important to note that because this is a social occurrence, this belief is widely held—it is the opinion of a significantly large portion of the population.

At some point in time, there may have been evidence of certain group characteristics that developed into a stereotyped belief. Therefore, some of the stereotyped characteristics may apply, such as typical symptoms that individuals with mood disorders may be experiencing. However, many of these characteristics would not. Frequently, stereotypes are developed in an effort to explain events or circumstances that are not fully understood. Unfortunately, even when better explanations, such as scientific evidence, are offered, stereotypes often linger.

Let us look at some of the more prevalent examples. One common stereotype of people with mood disorders is that they are "weak and lazy." This stems from the uneducated belief that people could help themselves "if they really wanted to." However, we now know that this explanation is an incredibly simple one that all scientific evidence negates. Such an explanation does not take into account the three perspectives presented in Chapter 5 (the biomedical, the behavioral, and the analytical). For instance, can we accuse individuals with mood disorders of not helping themselves get better if they have a chemical imbalance that requires medication? And if these individuals take medication, can we accuse them of being weak? After having been appropriately informed, this stereotype seems quite unfair and silly.

Another stereotype is that people who suffer from mood disorders will never get better. This stereotype also stems from ancient times, when adequate treatments were not an option. Without the knowledge of what mood disorders are and how to treat them, sufferers could not be helped. Rather, they were condemned because of society's ignorance. Today, with a more comprehensive understanding of mood disorders, sufferers can be suitably diagnosed and treated. They do not have to suffer for the rest of their lives.

Yet another stereotype is that individuals with mood disorders are "strange, weird, or different." Again, when mood disorders were not understood, sufferers were ostracized, condemned, and treated harshly. This would naturally make anyone who is already in pain act "differently." In addition, insufficient treatment would allow the abnormal behaviors to continue. However, we now know that certain symptoms of mood disorders can make individuals behave in maladaptive ways, but that is a condition of the disorder.

Think about how you act when you are in some type of pain—for instance, when you have the flu or have a bad headache. Do you act the same as you normally would?

Probably not, but this does not mean that you are strange or different in some way. Furthermore, some of the world's most popular and well-respected people have suffered from mood disorders. A few examples of these people include Marilyn Monroe, Hans Christian Andersen, Vincent van Gogh, Ernest Hemingway, Charles Dickens, Michelangelo, Axl Rose, Ted Turner, Barbara Bush, Dick Clark, Francis Ford Coppola, Eric Clapton, Mike Wallace. . . the list goes on.[2] These people are not considered to be "weird!"

Fortunately, these stereotypes are not given as much credence as they once were. Society has come to look at mood disorders with new perspectives based on the current level of knowledge. Still, these stereotypes continue to linger to a lesser degree.

Guns N' Roses lead singer Axl Rose (center) suffered from a mood disorder.

Demographics of Mood Disorders

Stereotypes aside, mood disorders have very few boundaries. They affect individuals of all ages.[3] Cases have been detected as early as infancy, and as late as older adulthood. Where a person lives and how much money he or she has is equally unimportant in determining the presence of a mood disorder.[4] Although prevalence rates may differ according to gender (for unipolar but not bipolar mood disorders), both males and females are vulnerable to mood disorders.[5]

In addition, mood disorders are not limited to the Western societies. Investigators have found that mood disorders can be identified in all cultures.[6] It has also been found that the symptoms of the various mood disorders do not vary much among the different cultures.[7]

However, differences have been found in how the symptoms are experienced and expressed.[8] For example, a predominant feature of depression in the American culture is a produced feeling of sadness that is associated with guilt and self-deprecation. In European and other cultures, depression may be experienced as complaints pertaining to the body, such as headaches and stomach aches, or having a "broken heart." In Asian cultures, sufferers are more likely to express depression in terms of an "imbalance of the forces."

Furthermore, symptoms that are considered more "serious" or disturbing may vary from culture to culture. For example, here in the United States, sadness and grief are more likely to be considered a serious matter. In other cultures, irritability may be viewed as more problematic. In still other cultures, social withdrawal and isolation would be the most worrisome symptom.

Individualism Versus Collectivism

Part of what causes these variations in the expression of symptoms and in what is judged more or less serious has to do with a society's value system. For example, the American culture tends to value *individualism,* or forming an identity based on one's own merits or goals rather than the group's merits or goals. Therefore, depressive symptoms are more likely to cause self-depreciation in the United States than in other cultures that value collectivism (putting the group's goals ahead of one's personal goals). In a society that values collectivism, irritability or hostility toward others would be more disconcerting.

Therefore, the predominance of symptom expression may be largely determined by what is considered acceptable in a given society. This would help explain why prevalence rates of mood disorders fluctuate so much among the various cultures.[9] What is viewed as "normal" versus "abnormal" within the cultures influences clinical diagnosis and prevalence rates. Here in America, mood disorders are among the most commonly diagnosed disorders,[10] occurring in approximately one-eighth of the population.

Stress and Mood Disorders

At the beginning of this chapter, we mentioned that another reason why prevalence rates in America are so high might be because of the excessive demands and stresses placed on people in our society. In an individualistic society, it is frequently assumed that every individual must constantly strive for success at all costs. Unfortunately, what is often the first expense is one's own physical, mental, and emotional health.

High levels of stress can lead to an impaired ability to function effectively.[11] There is often a "domino effect" when this occurs—the person's ability to concentrate, perform, execute, and complete tasks is compromised, which leads to frustration. The person may become doubtful that he will ever get out from under all the demands and expectations placed on him, and may engage in negative thinking, such as guilt. Eventually, the two key features of depression (helplessness and hopelessness) may emerge. Therefore, the stress the person has felt has led to a mood disorder.

When people continue to push themselves to perform under these conditions, a syndrome known as *burnout* can occur. Burnout is the physical, mental, and emotional exhaustion of an individual who has been exposed to prolonged periods of emotionally demanding circumstances.[12] Burnout typically generates disinterest, irritability, fatigue, and emotional numbness. Instances of burnout have become increasingly common in our society. Again, this may have to do with the value placed on being useful, important, productive, and in general, individualistic.[13]

When burnout occurs, the downward spiral of depressive symptoms is brought about. Individuals who are engaged in such a spiral often end up with a full-blown depressive

A person suffering from stress may doubt that he will ever get out from under all the demands placed on him.

episode. The opposite can also happen—the individual may begin to act in an erratic, impulsive, and unpredictable manner that can eventually lead to a manic episode. This scenario is not as common, however.

Therefore, it is important to take precautions to reduce stress levels. Of course, we are only presenting the worst-case scenarios here—there are times when stress can lead to improved performance and success. However, this is true only when stress levels do not become excessive.

This chapter has been geared toward looking more closely at cultural variables in the development and diagnosis of mood disorders. We also uncovered some explanation of why prevalence rates have been consistently on the rise. In Chapter 8, we will investigate current trends in understanding mood disorders, and look at future considerations in coping with this incapacitating illness.

8

The Future and Mood Disorders

In 1874, Sir Francis Galton (1822–1911), a British scientist who was known for his research in meteorology, heredity, and anthropology, coined the term "nature versus nurture."[1] The nature-nurture controversy refers to the debate of heredity (nature) as opposed to the environment (nurture). Galton highlighted and magnified the age-old question of which is more critical in the development of a person's identity (personality, intelligence, unique characteristics, etc.)—one's inherited genes or one's emotional upbringing. Galton explained that nature refers to all with which one is born, while nurture is everything in one's environment that influences these natural tendencies by either strengthening them or reducing them.

This debate has continued for over a century with varying degrees of emphasis. Today, the nature-nurture controversy is still widely discussed. Using modern scientific techniques in combination with older ones, researchers have been trying to determine the answer to this dispute. An enormous amount of time, energy, and money has been poured into the deliberation of this very question over the last century.

Interestingly, what has come out of this research generally indicates that mood disorders can be attributed to an equal combination of nature and nurture.[2] Therefore, genetics generally contribute to 50 percent of a mental illness, and environmental influences contribute to the other 50 percent. This understanding aids in the diagnosis and treatment of mood disorders.

Psychobiological Research Trends and Family Studies

As mentioned earlier, there are many types of research studies that are currently in progress in an effort to further develop our understanding of mood disorders. Some of these studies fall under the category of *psychobiological research*,[3] which is the study of psychological occurrences in terms of their biological structure. Similarly, some of these studies fall under the heading of *behavioral genetics*,[4] which is a branch of psychobiology that is specifically geared to the investigation of genetic influences on behavior. This branch of psychobiology is focused more on the nature side of the nature-nurture debate, as genetics involve that with which one is born.

Family studies are also being conducted to further clarify genetic versus environmental influences on mood disorders.[5] These studies include research that evaluates the extent to which heredity influences human development. There are a few main ways that family studies can be conducted, some of which involve twin studies.

Twin studies are research that is conducted to assess the influence of heredity by analyzing identical or fraternal twins. Identical, or *monozygotic*, twins are twins who are born from one *zygote* (new cell that is produced when a sperm cell joins with an egg) that has split. Fraternal, or *dizygotic*, twins are the result of two zygotes that are fertilized separately, but at the same time. In researching mood disorders, identical twins who are brought up together can be compared with identical twins who are brought up apart, with different families or in different areas. Fraternal twins can be compared in the same way, as can siblings who are not twins.

Adoption studies are similar to twin studies. In adoption studies, the resemblances of adopted children and their adoptive parents are compared with those of their biological parents. Family *genograms* (diagrams of family trees containing all pertinent information) can also be used in an attempt to investigate the comparison between family genetics and environmental influences.

There is strong supporting evidence that genetics plays a large role in determining mood disorders.[6] This is especially true for the bipolar disorders, which may be more chemically and thus genetically based than the unipolar disorders,[7] although this, too, is still under investigation. Higher genetic resemblances often result in higher rates of emotional resemblance. For instance, the likelihood that both identical twins

81

Studies using identical twins, like these girls shown here, are helpful in researching mood disorders.

will experience Bipolar I Disorder is 33–90 percent, whereas it is about 50 percent for identical twins with Major Depressive Disorder.[8] However, fraternal twins are 5–25 percent more likely to share Bipolar I Disorder, while 10–25 percent of fraternal twins are more likely to have Major Depressive Disorder in common.[9]

However, the general opinion is that mood disorders are still at least partially due to one's environment.[10] At most, we can safely presume that some individuals may have a certain predisposition to mood disorders, and that their environment helps to nurture this predisposition. Naturally, however, each individual is unique in his or her own set of circumstances, so it is important to keep in mind that what may apply to the general population does not always apply to every person.

Neurochemistry, Psychopharmacology, and Alternative Medicines

Research regarding neurochemical pathways and biological chemistry is continually being investigated.[11] This research involves the study of *neurotransmitters*, which are cells that transmit, or signal, other cells. In addition to the three main neurotransmitters associated with mood disorders (serotonin, norepinephrine, and dopamine), other neurochemical factors are being investigated for their role in mood disorders.[12] These include *amino acid neurotransmitters*, a simple chemical within the body that acts as a transmitter; and *second-messenger systems*, the breakdown products of other neurotransmitters.[13]

Advances in science have also given us a whole new array of psychopharmacologic interventions for mood disorders.[14] Only as far back as two decades ago, there were very few medications from which to choose to treat mood disorders. Most of these had harsh side effects and needed to be taken several times a day. Today, there are a large variety of psychopharmacologic interventions for mood disorders.[15] Most of these have very few side effects and are longer-lasting. In fact, some medications for mood disorders only need to be taken once daily or even weekly.

In addition to the prescribed medications, new discoveries in alternative treatments have extended the choices for people who suffer from mood disorders. Some examples include herbal and over-the-counter remedies, and acupuncture. However, these remedies should be used with caution because they have not been well-researched or approved by the Food and Drug Administration (FDA) the same way that prescribed medications have. In addition, alternative treatments are generally not monitored by professionals for adverse effects, which presents possible complications.

Recently, multiple studies have found that exercise is a highly beneficial treatment for depressed mood.[16] Although exercise has always been viewed as an important part of general health, research has found that chemical changes occur within the human body when a regimen of exercise is followed. Exercise helps to elevate and stabilize mood.[17] In addition, people who exercise are more likely to feel productive, effective, and better about themselves when they participate in a weekly exercise routine. This can involve going for walks, going to the gym, practicing with videotapes at home, or taking classes in aerobics, yoga, or the like. Exercise is also a good stress-buster that can be used as a healthy coping mechanism. All these benefits could potentially help alleviate the symptoms of mood disorders.

Psychotherapeutic Trends

Modern approaches to psychotherapy have made it more convenient for sufferers of mood disorders to get help. The current trend in psychotherapeutic practice is to limit the amount of time spent in treatment. Recent research has shown that short-term or time-limited psychotherapy can be as

A good exercise routine can help stabilize and elevate mood.

effective as taking medication.[18] Gone are the days of endless months and years of psychotherapy. Rather, the treatment of mood disorders has become focused on symptom reduction and prevention. Prevention can involve working toward the development of better coping skills, learning what triggers a depressive or manic episode, and learning to recognize the beginning signs of an episode.

Because psychotherapy has become more time-limited, it has also become less costly. This means that it has become more accessible to sufferers of mood disorders. Group therapy, as opposed to individual therapy, has also become more popular. It has been shown to be an effective treatment for some mood disorders.[19] Group therapy is also generally time-limited, focused on the treatment and prevention of mood disorders, and is more cost-effective. In addition, group therapy is a forum where people who suffer from mood disorders can express their feelings and listen to the thoughts of others who are going through similar experiences.

Psychotherapy has also become more interactive. Modern approaches invite the patient to be an active participant in the planning and implementation of treatment goals. The patient is therefore given more of an opportunity to feel productive, useful, and capable of completing tasks. These benefits of modern approaches of psychotherapy are ideal in combating the symptoms of mood disorders.

We have presented only a few of the modern advances in dealing with mood disorders. Fortunately, research has been on the rise and new discoveries are continually being made.

Scientific studies will enable ongoing developments in psychopharmacotherapy. In addition, findings related to both the biological and environmental aspects of mood disorders will aid in the self-help techniques of sufferers. These efforts, in combination with a refined approach to behavioral medicine, will enhance the treatment options available to individuals with mood disorders.

In the beginning of this book, we presented the case illustration of Heather. By recognizing her symptoms, we began to understand how devastating and crippling mood disorders can be if left untreated. However, we were also able to see that, with the proper help and appropriate treatment, Heather would likely recover in just a matter of time. Just like Heather, there is hope for all sufferers of mood disorders.

Q&A

Q. Can I catch a mood disorder from someone else?

A. No. Mood disorders are not contagious, although there is evidence that links them genetically to other family members.

Q. Do young people suffer from mood disorders?

A. There have been cases of mood disorders found as early as in infancy, and as old as older adulthood.

Q. Do certain parts of the world have a higher occurrence of mood disorders than others?

A. Mood disorders are found in all societies in the world, although the way symptoms are expressed vary from culture to culture.

Q. Does a special diet or exercise help if you have a mood disorder?

A. It is always a good idea to eat healthy, but there is no special diet to help alleviate the symptoms of a mood disorder. However, studies have shown that exercise helps elevate and stabilize mood because chemical changes occur in the body when an exercise routine is followed.

Q. Are mood disorders fatal?

A. Unfortunately, the suicide rates rise dramatically for people who suffer from depressive episodes. However, with proper treatment, there is hope for all sufferers of mood disorders.

Q. Are there any cures for mood disorders?

A. There are many medications available today to treat the symptoms of mood disorders. Group or individual therapy has also proved effective in identifying the onset of a depressive or manic episode.

Mood Disorders Timeline

c. 460–1450 B.C.—Hippocrates, one of the great scientists in history, believes that melancholia (depression) is caused by an excess of black bile, a liver secretion. This idea remains influential until the 1800s.

A.D. 1000–1450—Exorcism is used to treat mental illness, which is then viewed as insanity or possession.

1450–1600—Witch-hunts are popular because it is believed that witches summon evil spirits that cause an individual to become "mad," or mentally ill.

1829—In a book by Robert Gooch, disorders that affect women in particular, such as postpartum depression, are delineated.

1880—Census distinguishes seven categories of mental illness, one of which is depression. Prior to this, official recordings of mental illnesses were lumped into one category, known as "idiocy/insanity."

1896—Emil Kraepelin names the disorder that had previously only been observed as manic-depressive psychosis (known today as bipolar disorder).

1938—Electroconvulsive therapy is used to treat psychosis in schizophrenia and mood disorders.

1940s—Lithium is used to quiet the symptoms of mania and later becomes one of the chief pharmacologic treatments of bipolar disorder.

1950s—The first *Diagnostic and Statistical Manual of Mental Disorders* (DSM) is published, which includes the diagnoses of Depressive Reaction, Cyclothymic Personality Disorder, Manic-Depressive Reaction, and Psychotic Depressive Reaction—all related to disorders of mood.

1951—Tofranil is found to be useful in treating depression.

1980s—Stereotypes regarding depression begin to wane.

1987—The *Diagnostic and Statistical Manual of Mental Disorders*, Third Edition (DSM-III) is published, and formally changes the name of Manic-Depressive Disorder to Bipolar Disorder.

1990s—More than 100,000 cases of mood disorders per year are treated with electroconvulsive therapy.

Present—New medications, treatments, and understandings continue to develop as mood disorders are continually being researched.

Glossary

abandonment—Feelings of being left behind or unattended.

alleviate—To improve or make better; to take away pain.

apprehension—Fear or uncertainty of what may come in the future.

compromise—An agreement reached by each side changing or giving up some demands.

conflict—A term used to describe two competing forces.

culture—A certain stage, form, or kind of civilization.

dementia—A condition of deteriorated mentality, often with emotional indifference.

despair—A feeling of complete hopelessness.

excessive—More than is necessary.

fluctuation—To change continually, especially up and down.

frequent—Repeated or occurring in short intervals.

frustration—Discouragement or defeat.

impair—To make less (as in value or strength) or worse.

inappropriate—Not suitable.

inhibition—Prevention or holding back from doing something.

intensity—The degree or amount of a strength or force.

intolerable—Unbearable.

irrational—Not based on reason.

irritable—Easily bothered or angered.

isolation—Being placed or kept apart from others.

malfunction—To break down or work improperly.

perceive—To obtain an awareness or understanding of something.

persistent—Continuing to act or exist longer than usual.

predispose—To affect or make susceptible to in advance.

recklessness—Wild, careless behavior.

recurrent—Appearing over and over again.

restraint—Control over one's thoughts or feelings.

severity—Harshness.

society—A group of people viewed as a community.

susceptible—Having little resistance.

tendency—Leaning toward a particular thought or action.

unconscious—Not intentional or planned.

unique—Unusual.

uterus—The organ of a female mammal in which the young develop before birth.

vulnerable—Open to attack or damage.

withdrawal—To pull away from others.

For More Information

The Alliance for the Mentally Ill/Friends and
Advocates of the Mentally Ill
432 Park Avenue South, #710
New York, NY 10016-8013
(212) 684-3264 (Help Line)

Depression Awareness, Recognition, and Treatment
National Institute of Mental Health
5600 Fishers Lane
Rockville, MD 20857
(800) 421-4211

National Alliance for the Mentally Ill (NAMI)
200 North Glebe Road, Suite 1015
Arlington, VA 22203
(800) 950-6264

National Depressive and Manic Depressive Association
(NDMDA)
730 North Franklin Street
Chicago, IL 60610
(800) 826-3632
http://www.ndmda.org

National Foundation for Depressive Illness, Inc. (NAFDI)
P.O. Box 2257
New York, NY 10116
(800) 248-4344
http://www.depression.org

National Institute of Mental Health (NIMH)
6001 Executive Boulevard
Rockville, MD 20892
(301) 443-4513
http://www.nimh.nih.gov

National Mental Health Association (NMHA)
1021 Prince Street
Alexandria, VA 22314
(800) 969-6642
http://www.nmha.org

Chapter Notes

Chapter 1. The Story of Heather

1. C. J. Murray and A. D. Lopez, "Evidence-based Health Policy—Lessons From the Global Burden of Disease Study," *Science*, November 1996, pp. 740–743.

2. National Foundation for Depressive Illness, Inc., "A Biochemical Illness," <http://www.depression.org/biochem.html> (June 3, 2002).

3. National Depressive and Manic-Depressive Association, "About Mood Disorders," <http://www.ndmda.org/aboutmood.html> (June 3, 2002).

4. S. Nolen-Hoeksema and S. J. Gurgus, "The Emergence of Gender Differences in Depression During Adolescence," *Psychological Bulletin*, May 1994, pp. 422–424.

5. M. L. Rutter, "Child Psychiatry: The Interface Between Clinical and Developmental Research," *Psychological Medicine*, February 1986, pp. 151–169.

6. American Psychiatric Association, *Diagnostic and Statistical Manual of Mental Disorders*, Fourth Edition, Text Revision (Washington, D.C.: American Psychiatric Association, 2000), pp. 345–428.

7. K. S. Kendler, "Genetic Epidemiology in Psychiatry: Taking Both Genes and Environment Seriously," *Archives of General Psychiatry*, November 1995, pp. 895–899; and R. Plomin, "Beyond Nature vs. Nurture," L. L. Hall, ed., *Genetics and Mental Illness: Evolving Issues for Research and Society*, (New York: Plenum Press, 1996), pp. 29–50.

Chapter 2. What Is a Mood Disorder?

1. H. I. Kaplan and B. J. Sadock, *Synopsis of Psychiatry*, Eighth Edition (Baltimore, Md.: Williams and Wilkins, 1998), p. 214.

2. American Psychiatric Association, *Diagnostic and Statistical Manual of Mental Disorders*, Fourth Edition, Text Revision (Washington, D.C.: American Psychiatric Association, 2000), pp. 345–428.

3. Kaplan and Sadock, pp. 364–366; H. I. Kaplan and B. J. Sadock, *Clinical Psychiatry*, (Baltimore, Md.: Williams and Wilkins, 1988), pp. 139–141; S. H. Kaplan, *Behavioral Science Notes* (USA, 1987), pp. 44–45; J. Preston and J. Johnson, *Clinical Psychopharmacology Made Ridiculously Simple*, Third Edition (Miami, Fla.: MedMaster, Inc., 1990) p. 2; W. Weiten, *Themes and Variations*, Fourth Edition (Pacific Grove, Calif.: Brooks/Cole Publishing Co., 1998), pp. 578–581; and American Psychiatric Association, pp. 345–428.

4. G. W. Brown, T. O. Harris, and C. Hepworth, "Life Events and Endogenous Depression: A Puzzle Reexamined," *Archives of General Psychiatry*, July 1994, pp. 525–534; and R. E. Ingram, J. Miranda, and Z. V. Segal, *Cognitive Vulnerability to Depression* (New York: Guilford Press, 1998), pp. 525–534.

5. W. Weiten, *Themes and Variations*, Fourth Edition (Pacific Grove, Calif.: Brooks/Cole Publishing Co., 1998), pp. 519–523.

6. M. E. Seligman, *Learned Optimism* (New York: Alfred A. Knopf, 1991), audiocassette.

7. L. Y. Abramson, M. E. Seligman, and J. D. Teasdale, "Learned Helplessness in Humans: Critique and Reformulation," *Journal of Abnormal Psychology*, February 1978, pp. 49–74; and M. E. Seligman, "Depression and Learned Helplessness," R. J. Friedman and M. M. Katz, ed., *The Psychology of Depression: Contemporary Theory and Research* (New York: Wiley, 1974), pp. 49–74.

8. Abramson, Seligman, and Teasdale, pp. 49–74; and Kaplan, *Behavioral Science Notes*, pp. 44–45.

9. W. Kalat, *Biological Psychology*, Sixth Edition (New York: Brooks/Cole Publishing Co., 1998), pp. 420–425.

10. J. Hopkins, M. Marcus, and S.B. Campbell, "Postpartum Depression: A Critical Review," *Psychological Bulletin*, May 1984, pp. 498–515.

11. Kaplan and Sadock, pp. 90–93.

12. R. Plomin, J. C. DeFries, G. E. McClearn, and M. Rutter, *Behavioral Genetics*, Third Edition (New York: W.H. Freeman, 1997); and Kaplan and Sadock, pp. 542–543.

13. Plomin, DeFries, McClearn, and Rutter; and Kaplan and Sadock, pp. 542–543.

Chapter 3. Types of Mood Disorders

1. H. I. Kaplan and B. J. Sadock, *Synopsis of Psychiatry*, Eighth Edition (Baltimore, Md.: Williams and Wilkins, 1998), pp. 542–543.

2. American Psychiatric Association, *Diagnostic and Statistical Manual of Mental Disorders*, Fourth Edition, Text Revision (Washington, D.C.: American Psychiatric Association, 2000), pp. 345–428.

3. D. N. Klein, P. M. Lewinsohn, and J. R. Seeley, "Psychosocial Characteristics of Adolescents With a Past History of Dysthymic Disorder: Comparison With Adolescents With Past Histories of Major Depressive and Non-Affective Disorders, and Never Mentally Ill Controls," *Journal of Affective Disorders*, February 1997, pp. 127–135.

4. American Psychiatric Association, pp. 345–428.

5. J. Angst, F. Angst, and H. H. Stassen, "Suicide Risk in Patients With Major Depressive Disorder," *Journal of Clinical Psychiatry*, vol. 60 (sup.), 1999, pp. 57–62.

6. American Psychiatric Association, pp. 345–428.

7. Ibid.

8. C. Z. Garrison, C. L. Addy, K. L. Jackson, R. E. McKeown, and J. L. Waller, "Major Depressive Disorder and Dysthymia in Young Adolescence," *American Journal of Epidemiology*, May 1992, p. 135.

9. Kaplan and Sadock, pp. 547–548.

10. American Psychiatric Association, pp. 345–428.

11. Ibid.

12. Ibid.; and Kaplan and Sadock, pp. 547–548.

13. American Psychiatric Association, pp. 345–428.

14. Ibid.

15. Ibid.

16. W. Coryell, J. Endicott, and M. Keller, "Rapidly Cycling Affective Disorder: Demographics, Diagnosis, Family History, and Course," *Archives of General Psychiatry*, February 1992, pp. 126–131.

17. American Psychiatric Association, pp. 345–428.

18. Ibid.; and R. H. Howland and M. E. Thase, "A Comprehensive Review of Cyclothymic Disorder," *Journal of Nervous Mental Disorders*, August 1993, p. 181.

19. American Psychiatric Association, pp. 345–428.

Chapter 4. Symptoms and Diagnosis

1. L. Y. Abramson, M. E. Seligman, and J. D. Teasdale, "Learned Helplessness in Humans: Critique and Reformulation," *Journal of Abnormal Psychology*, February 1978, pp. 49–74; and J. H. Wright and A. T. Beck, "Cognitive Therapy of Depression: Theory and Practice," *Hospital Community Psychiatry*, December 1993, pp. 1119–1127.

2. S. H. Kaplan, *Behavioral Science Notes* (USA, 1987), p. 44.

3. W. Weiten, *Themes and Variations*, Fourth Edition (Pacific Grove, Calif.: Brooks/Cole Publishing Co., 1998), pp. 578–581.

4. D. N. Klein, P. M. Lewinsohn, and J. R. Seeley, "Psychosocial Characteristics of Adolescents With a Past History of Dysthymic Disorder: Comparison With Adolescents With Past Histories of Major Depressive and Non-Affective Disorders, and Never Mentally Ill Controls," *Journal of Affective Disorders*, February 1997, pp. 127–135; and C. Segrin and L. Y. Abramson, "Negative Reactions to Depressive Behaviors: A Communication Theories Analysis," *Journal of Abnormal Psychology*, November 1994, pp. 655–668.

5. B. Birmaher, N. D. Ryan, D. E. Williamson, D. A. Brent, J. Kaufman, R. E. Dahl, J. Perel, and B. Nelson, "Childhood and Adolescent Depression: A Review of the Past Ten Years, Part I,"

Journal of the American Academy of Child and Adolescent Psychiatry, November 1996, pp. 1427–1439; and I. Kolvin, M. L. Barrett, S. R. Bhate, T. P. Berney, O. O. Famuyiwa, T. Fundudis, and S. Tyrer, "The Newcastle Child Depression Project: Diagnosis and Classification of Depression," *British Journal of Psychiatry* (sup.), 1991, pp. 9–21.

    6. H. I. Kaplan and B. J. Sadock, *Synopsis of Psychiatry*, Eighth Edition (Baltimore, Md.: Williams and Wilkins, 1998), p. 365.

    7. American Psychiatric Association, *Diagnostic and Statistical Manual of Mental Disorders*, Fourth Edition, Text Revision (Washington, D.C.: American Psychiatric Association, 2000), pp. 345–428.

    8. Ibid.; Kaplan and Sadock, pp. 368–371; and S. H. Kaplan, pp. 43–44.

    9. B. Geller, B. Zimerman, M. Williams, M. P. DeBello, J. Frazier, and L. Beringer, "Phenomenology of Prepubertal and Early Adolescent Bipolar Disorder: Examples of Elated Mood, Grandiose Behaviors, Decreased Need for Sleep, Racing Thoughts, and Hypersexuality," *Journal of Child and Adolescent Psychopharmacology* (sup.), 2002, pp. 3–9.

    10. S. H. Kaplan, pp. 44–45.

    11. Geller, Zimerman, Williams, DeBello, Frazier, and Beringer, pp. 3–9.

Chapter 5. Treatment of Mood Disorders

    1. K. E. Poroquet, "Status of Treatment of Depression," *South Medical Journal* (sup.), 1999, pp. 846–856.

    2. R. J. Corsini and D. Wedding, *Current Psychotherapies* (Itasca, Ill.: F. E. Peacock Publishers, Inc., 1995), pp. 107–113; W. Weiten, *Themes and Variations*, Fourth Edition (Pacific Grove, Calif.: Brooks/Cole Publishing Co., 1998), pp. 607–625; and R. Ewen, *An Introduction to Theories of Personality* (Hillsdale, N.J.: Lawrence Erlbaum Associates, 1988), pp. 51–56.

    3. Ibid.

    4. Ibid.

5. Ibid.

6. Ibid.

7. J. H. Wright and A. T. Beck, "Cognitive Therapy of Depression: Theory and Practice," *Hospital Community Psychiatry*, December 1993, pp. 1119–1127.

8. W. Z. Potter and M. V. Rudorfer, "Electroconvulsive Therapy—A Modern Medical Procedure (Editorial)," *New England Journal of Medicine*, March 1993, pp. 882–883; and W. Z. Potter, M. V. Rudorfer, and H. Manji, "The Pharmacologic Treatment of Depression," *New England Journal of Medicine*, August 1991, pp. 633–642.

9. C. B. Nemeroff, "Psychopharmacology of Affective Disorders in the Twenty-First Century," *Biological Psychiatry*, October 1998, pp. 517–525.

10. Potter, Rudorfer, and Manji, pp. 633–642.

11. Lithium Information Center, *Lithium and Manic Depression: A Guide* (University of Wisconsin, 1989).

12. Potter and Rudorfer, "Electroconvulsive Therapy—A Modern Medical Procedure (Editorial)," pp. 882–883.

13. R. C. Hermann, R. A. Dorwart, C. W. Hoover, and J. Brody, "Variation in ECT Use in the United States," American Journal of Psychiatry, June 1995, pp. 869–875.

14. J. G. Small, M. G. Klapper, J. J. Kellams, M. J. Miller, V. Milstein, P. H. Sharpley, and I. F. Small, "Electroconvulsive Treatment Compared With Lithium in the Management of Manic States," *Archives of General Psychiatry*, August 1988, pp. 727–732.

15. R. G. Vasile, J. A. Samson, J. Bemporad, K. L. Bloomingdale, D. Creasy, B. T. Fenton, J. E. Gudeman, and J. J. Schildkraut, "A Biopsychosocial Approach to Treating Patients With Affective Disorders," *American Journal of Psychiatry*, March 1987, pp. 341–344.

Chapter 6. The History of Mood Disorders

1. W. Weiten, *Themes and Variations*, Fourth Edition (Pacific Grove, Calif.: Brooks/Cole Publishing Co., 1998), pp. 578–581.

2. B. R. Hergenhahn, *An Introduction to the History of Psychology*, Third Edition (New York: Brooks/Cole Publishing Co., 1997), pp. 433–459.

3. W. B. Maher and B. A. Maher, "Psychopathology: II. From the Eighteenth Century to Modern Times," G. A. Kimble and K. Schlesinger, ed., *Topics in the History of Psychology* (Hillsdale, N.J.: Lawrence Earlbaum, 1985), pp. 251–294.

4. Hergenhahn, pp. 433–459.

5. Ibid.

6. Ibid.

7. Ibid.

8. Ibid.

9. Ibid.

10. Ibid.

11. Ibid.; J. P. Morrissey and H. H. Goldman, "Cycles of Reform in the Care of the Chronically Mentally Ill," *Hospital and Community Psychiatry*, August 1984, pp. 785–793.

12. Morrissey and Goldman, pp. 785–793.

13. Hergenhahn, pp. 433–459.

14. Ibid.

15. Ibid.

16. Morrissey and Goldman, pp. 785–793.

Chapter 7. Mood Disorders, Society, and Culture

1. Centers for Disease Control and Prevention, "Suicide Deaths and Rates Per 100,000," <http://www.cdc.gov/ncipc/data/us9794/suic.htm> (August 12, 2001).

2. K. Jamison, *Touched With Fire: Manic-Depressive Illness and the Artistic Temperament* (New York: The Free Press, 1996); Education Planet, "Depression—Its Causes and What You Can Do About It," <http://www.educationplanet.com> (June 3, 2002).

3. H. I. Kaplan and B. J. Sadock, *Synopsis of Psychiatry*, Eighth Edition (Baltimore, Md.: Williams and Wilkins, 1998), pp. 524–580.

4. Ibid.

5. American Psychiatric Association, *Diagnostic and Statistical Manual of Mental Disorders*, Fourth Edition, Text Revision (Washington, D.C.: American Psychiatric Association, 2000), pp. 345–428; National Institute of Mental Health, "Do You Suffer From a Mood Disorder? Or Do You Know Someone Who Does? Find Out More Here," <http://www.nimh.nih.gov/publicat/index.cfm> (June 3, 2002).

6. J. C. Ballenger, J. R. Davidson, Y. Lecrubier, D. J. Nutt, L. J. Kirmayer, J. P. Lepine, K. M. Lin, D. Tajim, and Y. Ond, "Consensus Statement on Transcultural Issues In Depression and Anxiety From the International Consensus Group on Depression and Anxiety," *Journal of Clinical Psychiatry* (sup), 2001, pp. 47–55.

7. Ibid.

8. American Psychiatric Association, pp. 345–428.

9. Ballenger, Davidson, Lecrubier, Nutt, Kirmayer, Lepine, Lin, Tajim, and Ond, pp. 47–55.

10. C. J. Murray and A. D. Lopez, "Evidence-Based Health Policy—Lessons From the Global Burden of Disease Study," *Science*, November 1996, pp. 740–743.

11. R. M. Sapolsky, "Stress, Glucocorticoids, and Damage to the Nervous System: The Current State of Confusion," *Stress*, July 1996, pp. 1–19; B. S. McEwen, "Protective and Damaging Effects of Stress Mediators," *New England Journal of Medicine*, January 1998, pp. 171–179.

12. W. Weiten, *Themes and Variations*, Fourth Edition (Pacific Grove, Calif.: Brooks/Cole Publishing Co., 1998), pp. 578–581.

13. Ibid.

Chapter 8. The Future and Mood Disorders

1. B. R. Hergenhahn, *An Introduction to the History of Psychology*, Third Edition (New York: Brooks/Cole Publishing Co., 1997), p. 273.

2. R. Plomin, "Beyond Nature vs. Nurture," L. L. Hall, ed., *Genetics and Mental Illness: Evolving Issues for Research and Society* (New York: Plenum Press, 1996), pp. 29–50.

3. H. I. Kaplan and B. J. Sadock, *Synopsis of Psychiatry*, Eighth Edition (Baltimore, Md.: Williams and Wilkins, 1998), pp. 539–543.

4. Ibid., pp. 136–139.

5. Ibid.; A. G. Cardno, F. V. Rijsdijk, P. C. Sham, R. M. Murray, and P. McGuffin, "A Twin Study of Genetic Relationships Between Psychotic Symptoms," *American Journal of Psychiatry*, April 2002, pp. 539–545; and P. H. Wender. S. S. Kety, D. Rosenthal, F. Schulsinger, J. Ortmann, and I. Lunde, "Psychiatric Disorders in the Biological and Adoptive Families of Adopted Individuals With Affective Disorders," *Archives of General Psychiatry*, October 1977, pp. 923–929.

6. Kaplan and Sadock, pp. 542–543; and Wender, Kety, Rosenthal, Schulsinger, Ortmann, and Lunde, pp. 923–929.

7. National Institute of Mental Health, "Depression," <http://www.nimh.nih.gov/publicat/depression> (June 3, 2002).

8. Ibid.

9. Ibid.

10. K. S. Kendler, "Genetic Epidemiology in Psychiatry: Taking Both Genes and Environment Seriously," *Archives of General Psychiatry*, November 1995, pp. 895–899; and R. Plomin, "Beyond Nature vs. Nurture," L. L. Hall, ed., *Genetics and Mental Illness: Evolving Issues for Research and Society* (New York: Plenum Press, 1996), pp. 29–50.

11. Kaplan and Sadock, pp. 97–122; C. B. Nemeroff, "Psychopharmacology of Affective Disorders in the Twenty-First Century," *Biological Psychiatry*, October 1998, pp. 517–525; D. C. Steffens and K. R. Krishnan, "Structural Neuroimaging and Mood Disorders: Recent Findings, Implications for Classification, and Future Directions," *Biological Psychiatry*, May 1998, pp. 705–712; and H. K. Mansi, W. C. Drevets, and D. S. Charney, "The Cellular Neurobiology of Depression," *National Medicine*, May 2001, pp. 541–547.

12. Kaplan and Sadock, pp. 97–122.

13. Ibid.; and Steffens and Krishnan, pp. 705–712.

14. Nemeroff, pp. 517–525; D. N. Osser, "A Systematic Approach to the Classification and Pharmacotherapy of Nonpsychotic Major Depression and Dysthymia," *Journal of Clinical Psychopharmacology*, April 1993, p. 13; J. Preston and J. Johnson, *Clinical Psychopharmacology Made Ridiculously Simple*, Third Edition (Miami, Fla.: MedMaster, Inc., 1990) pp. 2–22; and J. S. March and B. Vitiello, "Advances in Paediatric Neuropsychopharmacology: An Overview," *International Journal of Neuropsychopharmacology*, June 2001, pp. 141–147.

15. F. Dimeo, M. Bauer, I. Varahram, G. Proest, and U. Halter, "Benefits From Aerobic Exercise in Patients With Major Depression," *British Journal of Sports Medicine*, April 2000, pp. 114–117; and CNN.com, "Depression and Exercise," <http://www.cnn.com/2000/health/mayo/09/27/depression.exercise/index.html> (June 3, 2002).

16. Ibid.

17. K. Hopayian, "Non-directive Psychotherapy Versus Routine General Practitioner Care," *The Lancet*, December 6, 1997, pp. 1662–1665; and R. J. Derubeis, L. A. Gelfand, T. Z. Tang, and A. D. Simons, "Medications Versus Cognitive Behavior Therapy For Severely Depressed Outpatients: Mega-Analysis of Four Randomized Comparisons," *American Journal of Psychiatry*, July 1999, pp. 1007–1013.

Further Reading

Ayer, Eleanor H. *Everything You Need to Know About Depression.* New York: Rosen Publishing Group, Inc., 2001.

Curtiss, Arline. *Depression is a Choice: Winning the Fight Without Drugs.* New York: Hyperion Press, 2002.

Peacock, Judith. *Bipolar Disorder.* Mankato, Minn.: Capstone Press, Inc., 2000.

Smith, Linda Wasmer. *Depression: What It Is, How to Beat It.* Berkeley Heights, N.J.: Enslow Publishers, Inc., 2000.

Weaver, Robyn M. *Depression.* Farmington Hills, Mich.: Gale Group, 1998.

Internet Addresses

Psychology Information Online: Bipolar Disorder
<http://www.psychologyinfo.com/depression/bipolar.htm>

Teens for Teens: Help Stop Teenage Depression
<http://www.teensforteens.net/>

TeenTalk International: Depression
<http://www.teentalk.com/>

Index

Lithium, 57

M

Major Depressive Disorder, 11, 28–29, 82

maladaptive behavior, 53–54, 60, 72

mania, 7, 27
hypomania, 31
symptoms associated with, 43–49, 78

manic-depressive illness. *See* bipolar disorder

medical conditions, 17, 21–22, 32

medical examination, 32, 33, 49

medication, 55–57, 83–84

mental illness, historical explanations, 61–66

mixed state, 16

mood, definition, 15

mood disorders
comorbid, 30
overview, 7–8, 15–16, 26
spectrum of, 28
substance-induced, 32–34

mood stability, 43, 56–57, 84

motivation, lack of, 7, 9, 12, 39, 42

N

nature *vs.* nurture, 79–80, 82–83

neurochemicals, 22, 34, 83–84, 88

neurosis, hysterical, 66

norepinephrine, 22, 83

"normal," perception of, 60–61, 74–75

O

optimism, 44

organizations, 93–94

P

personal distress, 60

pessimism, 38

Pinel, Dr. Philippe, 67

political aspects, 60–61

postpartum depression, 22, 23

prevalence, 11, 70, 74, 75

prevention, 8, 86

productivity, drop in, 7, 11, 12–13, 42

prognosis, 24, 72

psychobiological research, 80–83

psychological explanation for mental illness, 66

psychopharmacologics. *See* medication

psychosis, 31

psychotherapy, 14, 50–53, 84, 86

R

recklessness, 48

research, 80–83

resources, 93–94, 109–110

S

sadness, 7, 8, 16, 74

scientific trends, 60–61

serotonin, 22, 83

sexual indiscretion, 48

shock therapy. *See* electroconvulsive therapy

Skinner, B. F., 53

sleep disturbances, 10, 22, 40, 44–45, 46